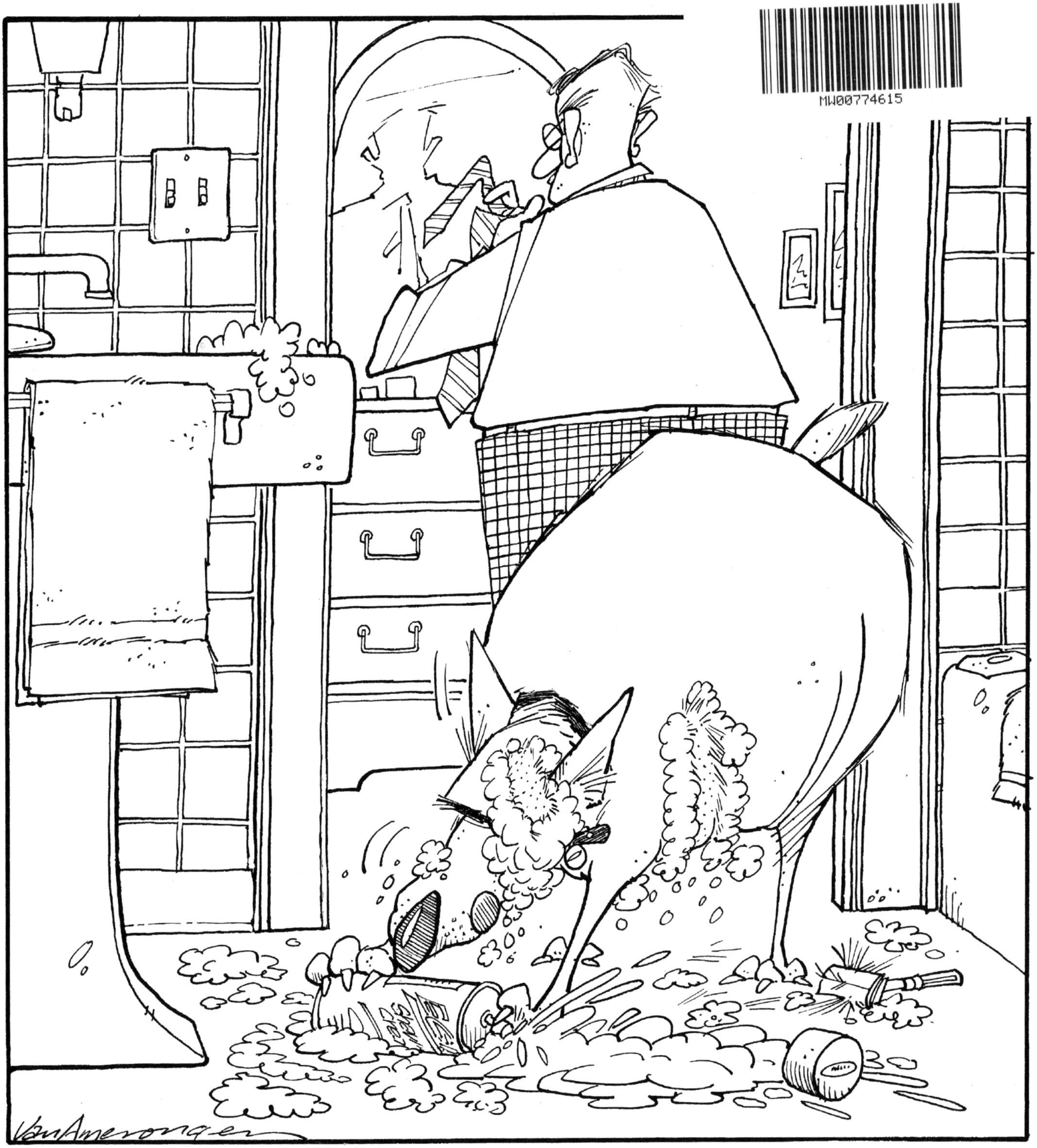
VanAmerongen

Cartoon Collections by Jerry Van Amerongen

Practicing People Skills

ON BALLARD STREET

The Comic Art of Jerry Van Amerongen

SYREN BOOK COMPANY   Minneapolis

Published by
Syren Book Company
5120 Cedar Lake Road
Minneapolis, MN 55416
763-398-0030
www.syrenbooks.com

Printed in the United States of America on acid-free paper

ISBN 978-0-929636-77-1

Library of Congress Catalog Card Number: 2007928523

Introduction

I'd like to thank my brother Don, who worked long hours and with much skill so this book could be presented to our publisher in a digital form. Thanks also to the good folks at Syren Book Company for their advice and craftsmanship.

The cartoons in this collection are from the years 2001 through 2005. I chose them because I liked them personally for one reason or another, and because they provided a balanced view of the content most often found in Ballard Street, the newspaper cartoon.

I'm often asked where my ideas come from. Much of the time I have a preconceived notion about what I want to illustrate, but just as often, I start with a miniature "scribble sketch" that slowly evolves into a complete scene. I might start with a facial expression, which then suggests a certain body posture. This overall expression could suggest a type of reaction, such as surprise or suspicion. So, I add an element to the drawing that could be causing such a reaction…how about a dog! By himself a dog isn't that compelling, but what if we added a lampshade to his head? This suggests an interior location, like a living room. In the background we might add a shade-less table lamp on the floor. Now we have a complete scene, and depending on what sort of personality our person suggests, we can arrive at a caption that rings true to the person's look, and to the other elements in the drawing.

I do this sort of sketching in school notebooks, and you will find several pages reproduced on pages 2 and 6 of this book. Notice also on page 2 the actual sketch of the dog practicing his people skills, which evolved into the finished cartoon on the title page, which evolved into the oil painting used for the cover. I must stop! I'm typing my fingertips numb. Thanks for buying this book (you are buying this book aren't you!)

Jerry Van Amerongen
Summer 2007

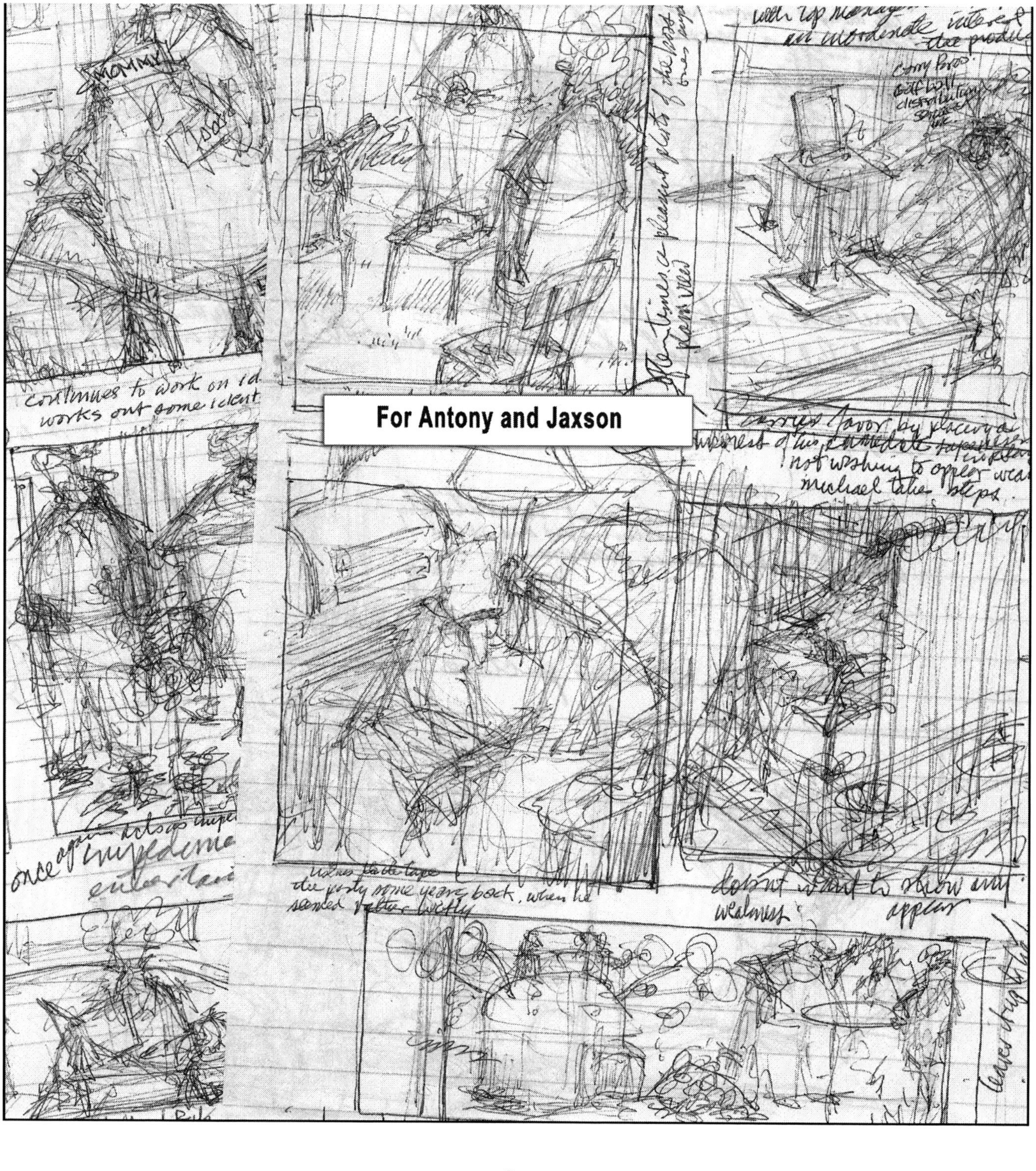
MOMMY
continues to work on id
works out some ident

For Antony and Jaxson

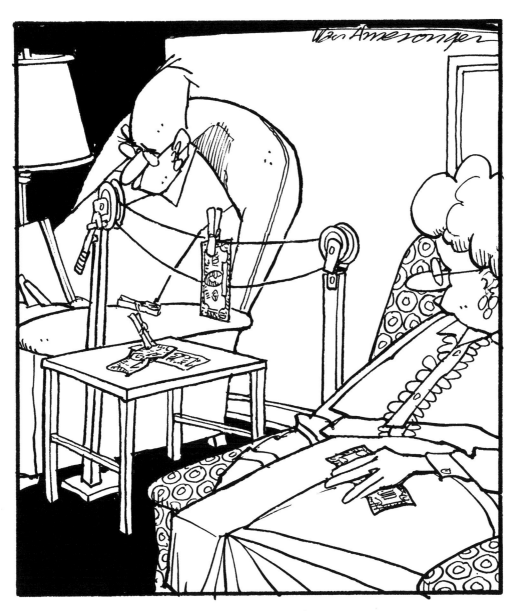

The Kirby's have money issues.

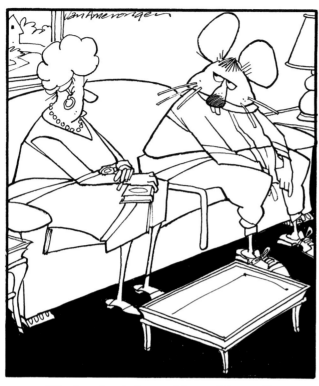

"Paul, nobody has a House Mascot!"

There are days, of course, when Spike wonders if he'll measure up.

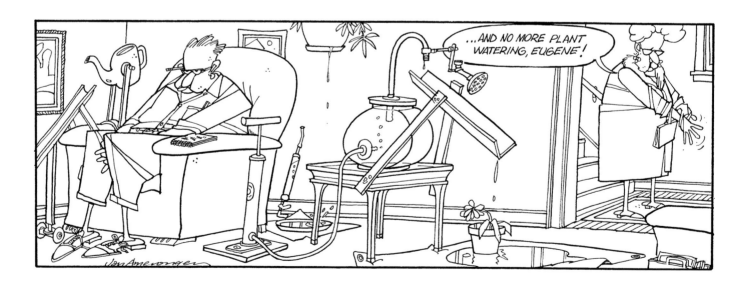

"Phyllis, have you ever wondered why I have a bad back?"

Stan begins his day with a small monetary transaction.

"Try wriggling some more!"

"I feel like I'm driving through life with a loose carburetor and a tank of bad gas."

"Not so close to the edge, Sparky!"

It's just that Marcia never thought Doug would settle on glue-making as a hobby.

"Tony, I've noticed you're beginning to scratch the furniture."

Subtlety · Nuance

IN YOUR FACE

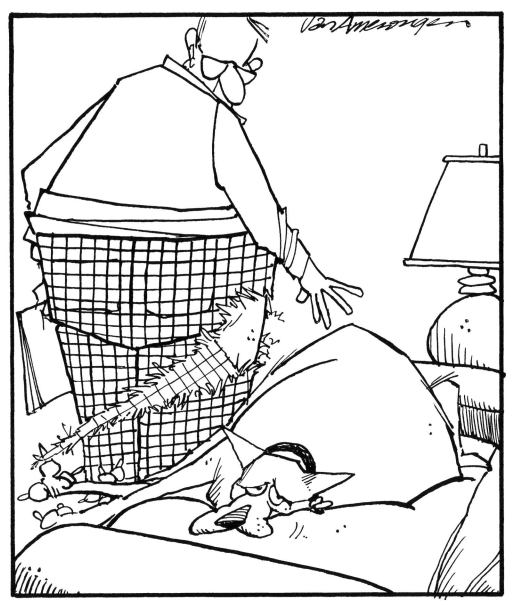

Thunder avails himself of a passing opportunity

Cory Middlebrooks has a small coal
deposit in his backyard.

How the Hemelshots can let their Miss Binky
go downtown unsupervised is a mystery.

It's a helpful reminder to Cynthia that she needs to think twice before remarrying.

"Now what?" frets Scooter.

Garrett's always trying to be so macho.

"So, you're saying, you do all the work."

Rudy takes a break to assess his chances
with Mr. Armbruster's electrical system.

Stern disciplinarian Dean Hartley confines himself to his room for the remainder of the day.

"You see, Sugar, we're at the very top of the pyramid as far as living things are concerned."

Beginner executive Chad Billingsley.

Bob exercises extremely poor judgment.

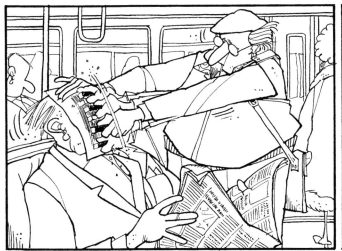

FACE
RUBBINGS
$2.00

It's an executive culture that's not right for everyone.

Like everyone else, Colin is fooling around with cloning.

"Perhaps Trudie is a better person than I am," thinks Thomas.

Mason advocates loose-fitting, less formal attire for men.

A small border skirmish breaks out between Bob and Ted.

"Arthur, it's your family!"

Gary builds shoes for a hobby.

"I'm not walking with you anymore, Tom!"

"Oh, for God's sake, Cliff!"

"More flora, my dear?"

"...And how long have you been putting little dog biscuits in your ear?"

TOBY! THERE YOU ARE!

LITTLE TOBY LOVES THE ROUGH AND TUMBLE LIFE

For Sparky, it's "alpha negativity" of the worst sort.

Whatever it takes, that's what Chad figures.

NO WONDER CHUCK OFTEN FINDS HIS SCOOTER PILED-UP AT THE BOTTOM OF THE DRIVE

Connie has been thinking, "If I limit my thinking,
would that extend the longevity of my thinking?"

If you wish to enter dance competitions with your pet, first decide who's going to lead.

Stu suspects Sally of enjoying a private joke he could well be the butt of.

Much to Fluffy's delight, the little puddle
she made on the front porch did freeze.

Claudia pursues her dream of someday
becoming a professional escape artist.

The Baxters are doing their part.

Damon and Hillary make handcrafted tugboats in their backyard.

"Don't go out there, Alex!"

"You've missed your peas completely, Michael!"

Carl's first move is a real doozy!

Roger and Darlene are visited by members of the humor committee.

Right away, Jason starts thinking about his own workload.

Sometimes, Sharon wonders if she isn't a great big secret she's keeping from herself.

ALLEN AND STEPHANIE ARE AGREED THEY MAY NEGATE ONE ANOTHER AT ANY TIME

"We'd like to send this next number out to the cute little cupcake at the corner table!"

"Well," thinks Courtney, "that's it for that!"

There are evenings when the stationary tubs
put Trevor in mind of the Merchant Marines.

Thomas likes to play "dump truck."

Of the Springer's, Roger Springer is the more withdrawn.

MR. CARSON, NONE OF US LIKE THE WAY THE QUARTER HAS GONE—BUT PLEASE, NO WEAPONS IN THE BOARDROOM!

Digger's day sours as Murray explains how he thinks they might be able to join the circus.

Penny does some deep cleaning.

Philip realizes the fancier the get-up, the
more likely it is people will believe you.

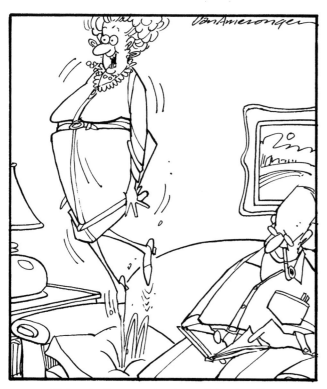

Vivian is the spark plug of the family.

"Morton, you were too playing with the fish!"

Connie's new pills are a godsend.

Muffin reaps the rewards for being
a very good kitty.

By twisting her head just so, Barb pinches off
small blood vessels in her neck, thus achieving
a faintly hallucinogenic state.

"It's a lovely day," thinks Teddy, "even with the beagle."

Orrin throws a very nice cross-body block.

TEA AND COOKIES ARE OFTEN AN IRKSOME BIT OF BUSINESS OVER AT THAD AND JANICE'S

By holding his fingers just so, Larry draws loose skin and ten years off his face.

Gary's hard on himself.

YOU HAVE PLENTY OF YOUR OWN AMENITIES, STEWART, MUST YOU BEGRUDGE MISS LU LU HER'S ?!

Chandler has misgivings about the new neighbor.

Buster likes to get the flavor of
his surroundings.

Small, personally-fitted muzzles help
reduce dysfunction in the household.

"Sure, there's a hundred million shapes out there, but is there other life?"

Roxanne can only hope for the day Neil turns mean and embittered.

SCOOTER TAKES IN A LITTLE DOMESTIC DUST-UP BETWEEN SANDY AND ROGER

With gravity's help, Hiram hopes to relocate certain body masses into his shoulders and chest.

For a change, Wally is having second thoughts.

"AS ALWAYS, ROSIE, CAREFUL WHAT YOU SAY"

The particular interests of the group leader have
a way of impacting other group members.

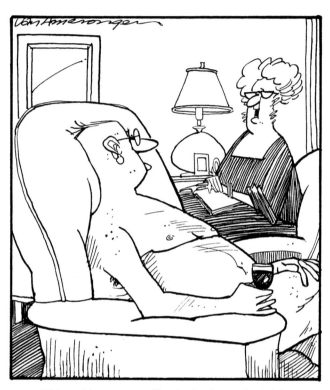

"Alex, I know you like to feel comfortable at home, but honestly!"

Stephen and Digger set out to see if they can scare up some lunch money.

Alex takes a first step off the beaten path.

"Edwin, I'm thinking of tinkering with my medication so I can communicate with you better.

THE LOOSE KNIT LITTLE CLUB KEEPS THEIR PIPES STASHED BEHIND HABNER'S GARAGE

Gordon uses poor business procedures.

"Some dogs", thinks Spike, "run with the wind and retrieve ducks, and stuff like that!".

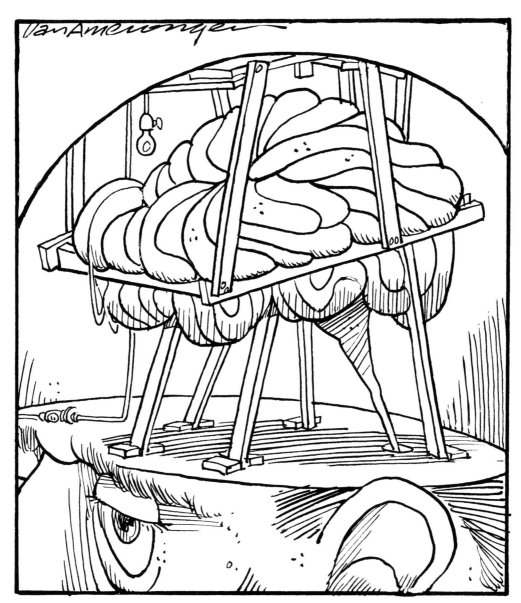

What it must look like to prop up the kind of
thinking we manage to come up with.

"I don't have any shoes, because you ate them!"

Kevin keeps a pain diary.

Another slow day for Chet and Rusty

Jesse is well on his way to doing nothing.

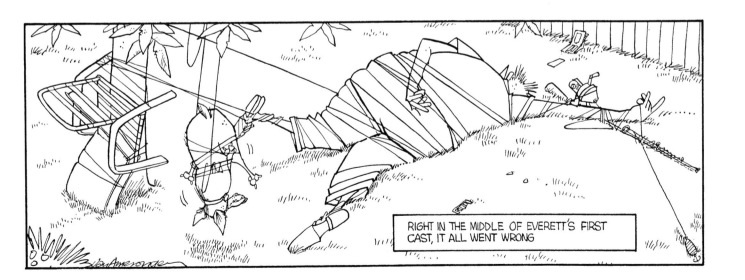

55

Even the possibility of water is
a fascination to Reggie.

There is a downside to living with an
aqueduct hobbyist..

More technological infidelity

Bus enthusiast Neil Ritchie

Janice and Todd Swenson keep a
detonation range in their backyard.

"So you see, Nelson, your socks did
survive my laundering as a pair!"

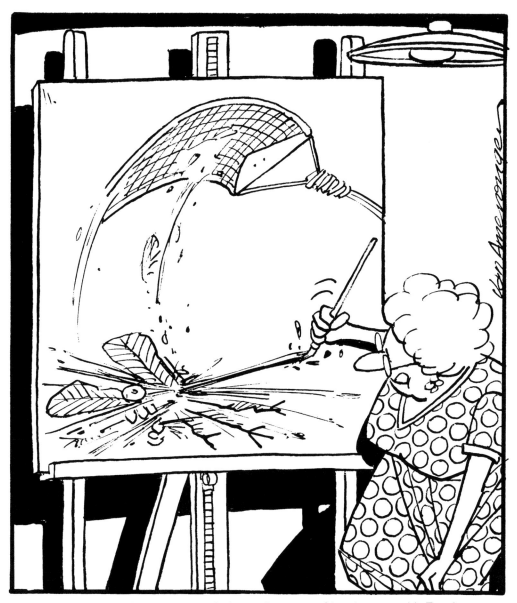

Ginger uses her art to work through some of her issues with Frank.

Chuck falls down the hill again!

After much pestering, Perry lets the Hamster drive.

Carson has misgivings about his moment of indiscretion.

"Roger, have you taken a good look at Yourself today?"

"You play 'How Much Is That Doggie In The Window' once, maybe twice, but three times and people start to look at you!"

ONCE AGAIN LITTLE ARTIE MANAGES TO FOUL MR. CARNEY'S FOWL

Herb is utterly without curiosity.

Neil enjoys spending time with other lovers of harness.

Then, just when Ben thought the neighbor's dog saw him as someone to fear...

What puzzles Ted is, just how many of these
little outbursts is he going to have this morning.

Rex and Stubby are a nuisance down at
Ted's Ham and Egger.

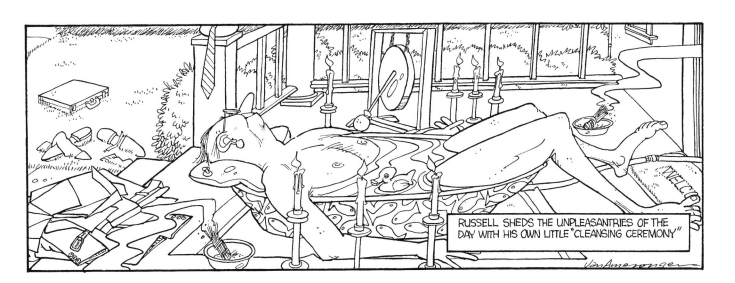

"Barrett, you were too in the pool!"

It's all getting a little scary for Stan.

Scooter cools off.

Arnie feels it allows him greater leeway with his fellow drivers.

Marcie makes little headway with her Ph.D. thesis, "The Specifics of Apathy.".

Another disappointing purchase from
Toby's Used Fountains.

Stan N. Newberry reconsidered.

OH SURE, THERE HAVE BEEN SMALL VICTORIES...BUT
WERE THERE REALLY THAT MANY?...AND AFTER ALL,
THEY WERE SMALL...

Doug's resentment builds as conversation continues without a single mention of a major Canadian city.

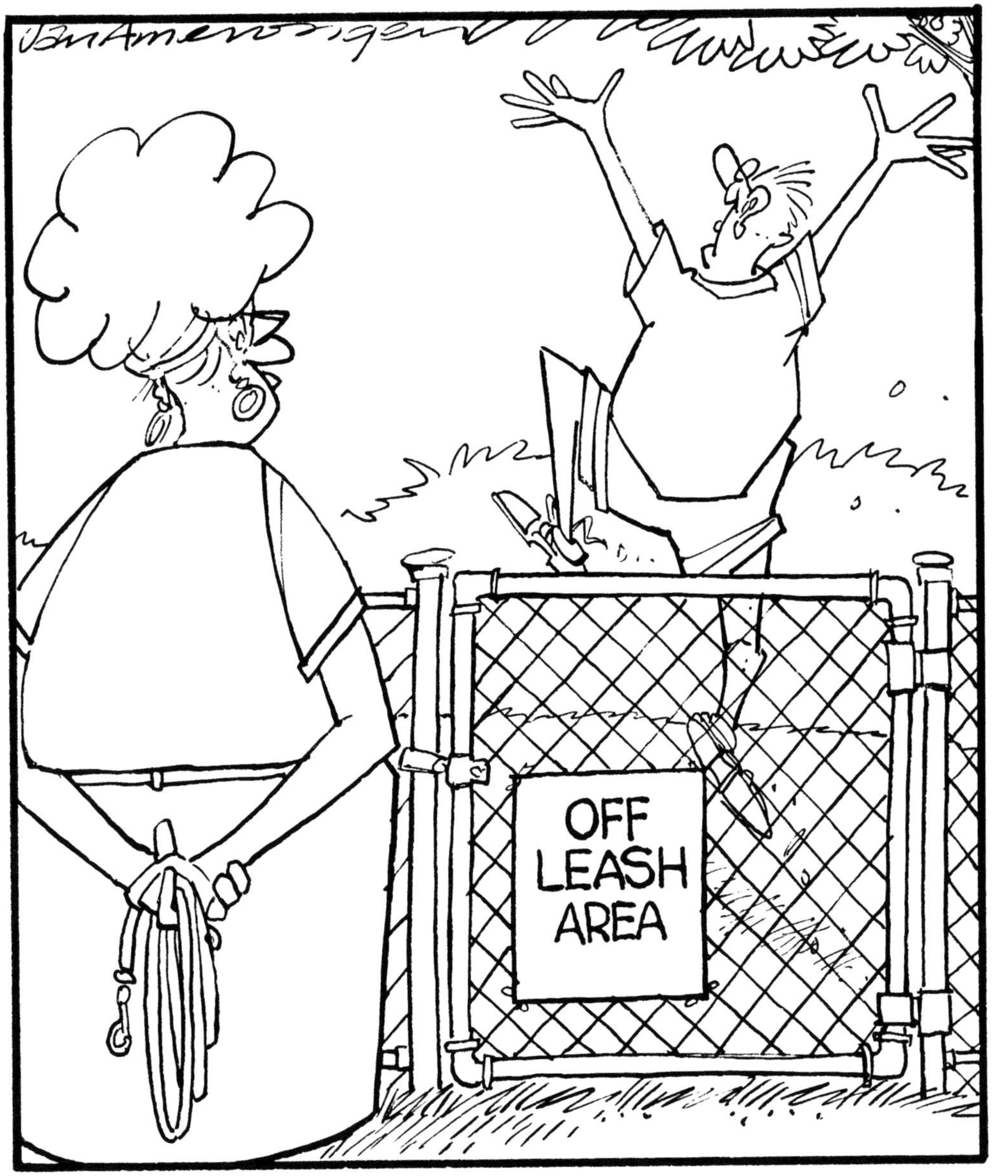
OFF
LEASH
AREA

Randy's argument is checked by Audrey.

"Roger, throwing yourself into the couch like that isn't going to help our finances."

Donald is easily distracted..

It's with a considerable degree of interest that Everett gazes over at the Wilson boy.

Nelson learns a hard lesson about keeping meat in his pocket.

Stewart suffers the consequences of losing the bulb in his left turn signal and having forever to turn right.

Perhaps it was the jostling of the car that
made things go all wrong for Bob.

"No, I won't hand you your hat, besides
get out of there!"

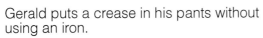
Gerald puts a crease in his pants without using an iron.

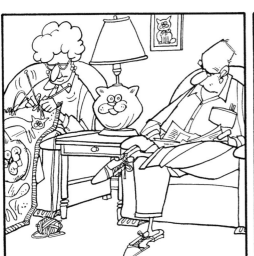

"You're having a good day, aren't you, Alice!"

The synchronized cell phones of Gwen and Trevor.

BOYD'S INCLUSIVE NATURE IS OFTEN A BURDEN TO THOSE AROUND HIM.

"You asked me last week where your razor was!"

Sandy went on line all by herself today.

Marcia's daily respite is enhanced by a
slow drip intravenous muscle relaxer.

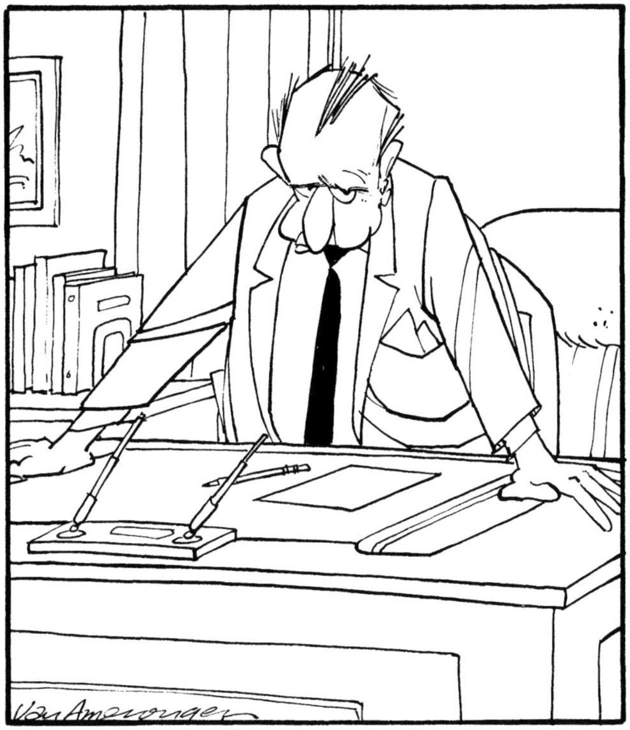

Nathan's beginning to wonder if his career isn't another thing that's making him feel inadequate.

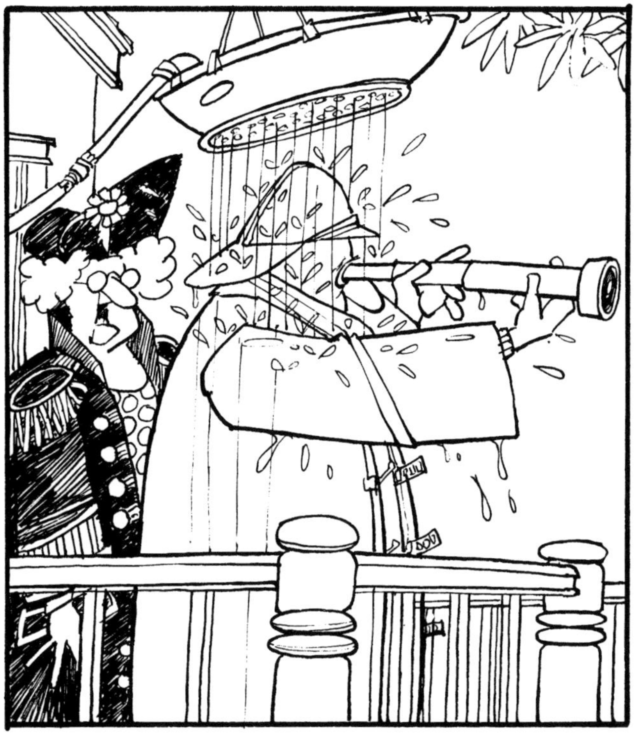

"Norman, when do I get to stand fast in stormy conditions?".

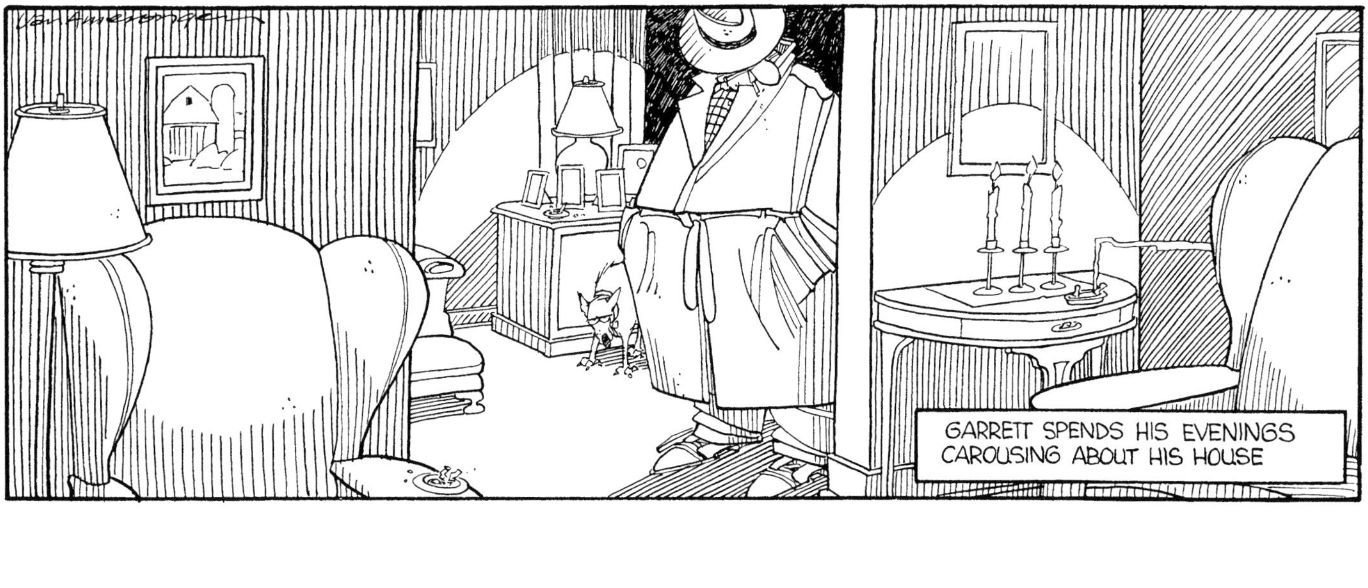
GARRETT SPENDS HIS EVENINGS CAROUSING ABOUT HIS HOUSE

"The head's all wrong!"

"While I'm less inclined to be overly upset with your sales projections, little Rufus seems to be more inclined!"

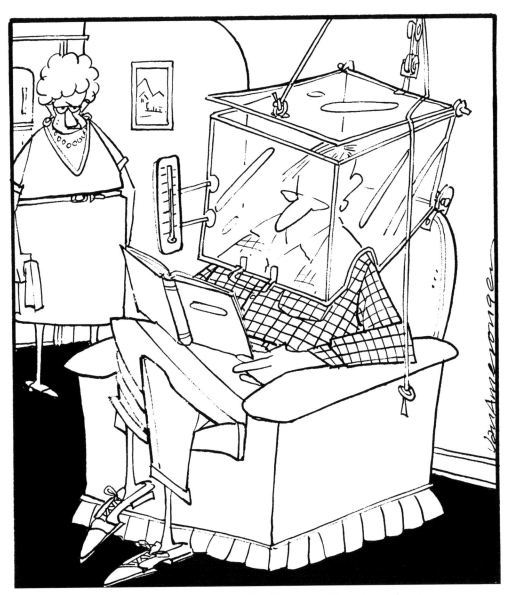

Chuck likes to rattle around in his own little microclimate.

"I said, I'm disappointed with the way you've been conducting yourself."

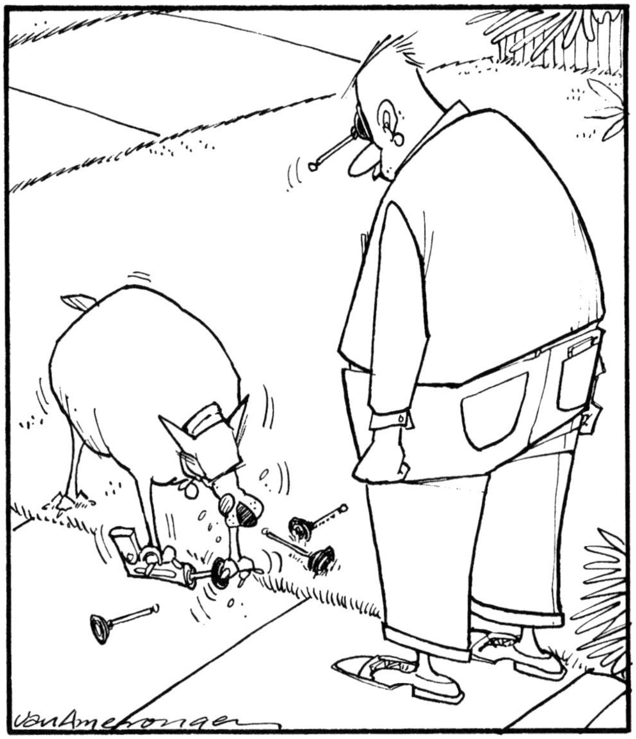

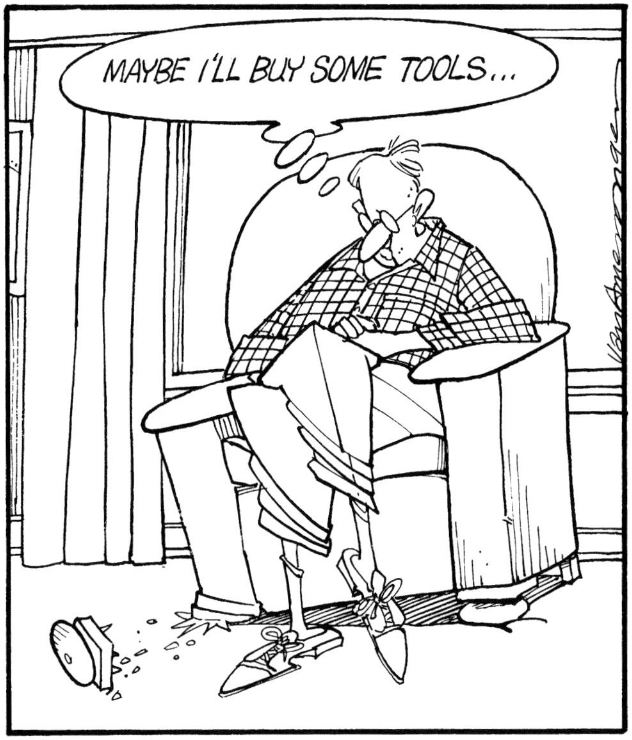
MAYBE I'LL BUY SOME TOOLS...

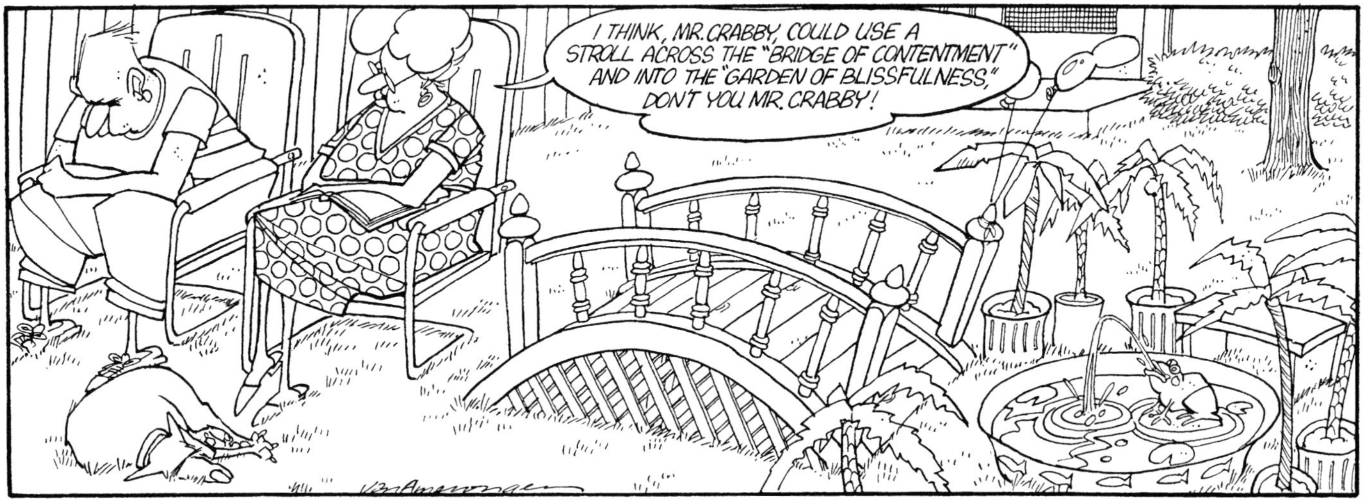
I THINK, MR. CRABBY, COULD USE A STROLL ACROSS THE "BRIDGE OF CONTENTMENT" AND INTO THE "GARDEN OF BLISSFULNESS," DON'T YOU MR. CRABBY!

"Yes, what is it?!"

"I said, watch out for the dump truck!"

Thad basks in the glow of a job well done.

Mr. Hurley likes to hold high ground
when he can.

"Yes, but is it a Windsor knot?!"

"Oh, geez, sorry!"

It acts as a constant reminder to Lance
not to play in the street.

Of course, once he put his glasses on,
Monty could see it wasn't a cat.

People amaze Stuffy. First off, they walk
around all day on their hind legs.

I SAID, SO YOU DECIDED AGAINST THE BLUE SPRUCE!

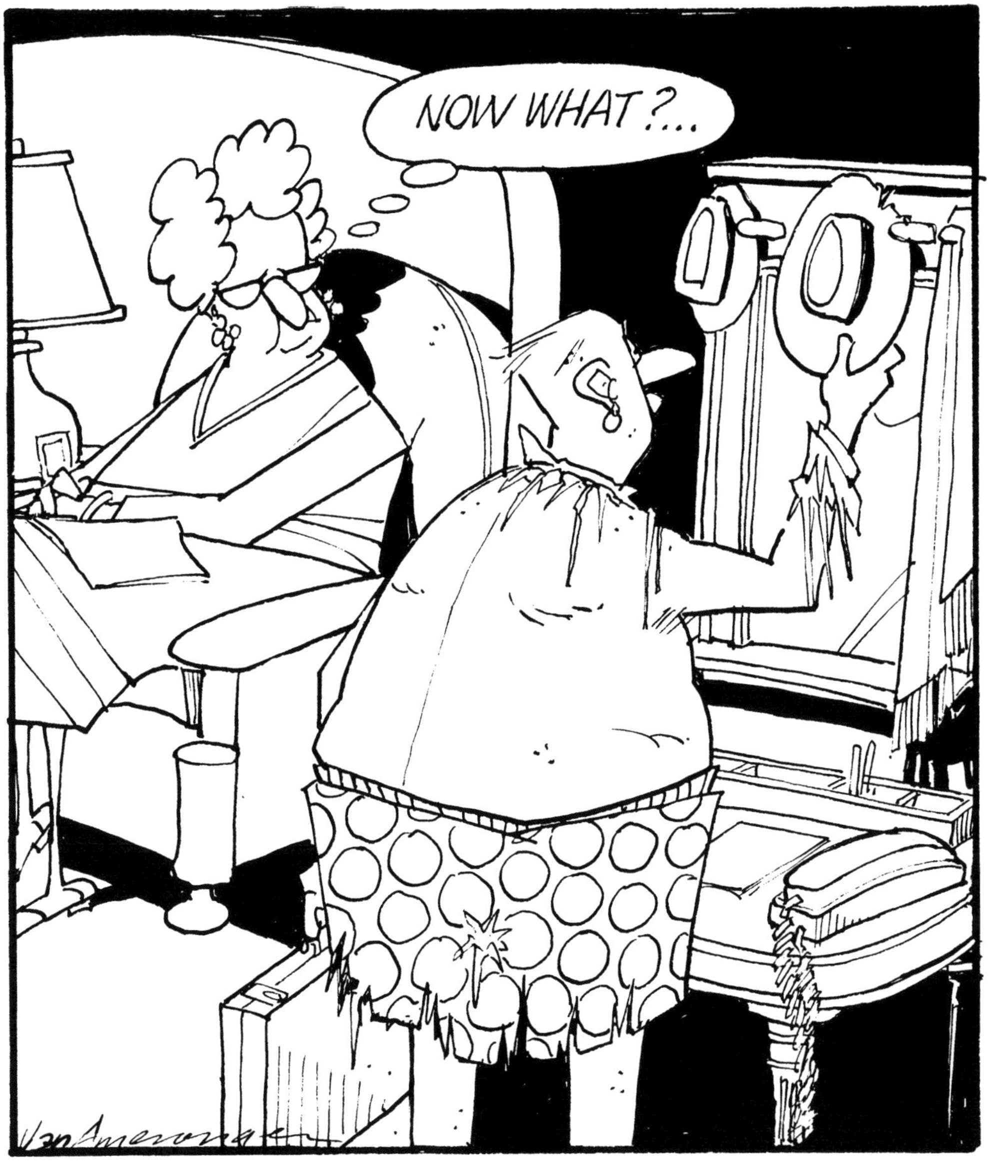
NOW WHAT?...

Mr. Kirby has yet to commit to the party.

Not only does little Toby mark his territory,
he marks everything passing through it.

Gloria's thinking she better start thinking of another good thought before a bad thought starts.

"Anybody we know?"

HI NEIGHBOR!

Roger is a purveyor of "niche knowledge."

It's Mrs. Starkey and an unencumbered Mr. Starkey.

THIS WASN'T WHAT BUD IMAGINED WHEN HIS NEIGHBOR FIRST TALKED ABOUT ORGANIZING A MEN'S GROUP

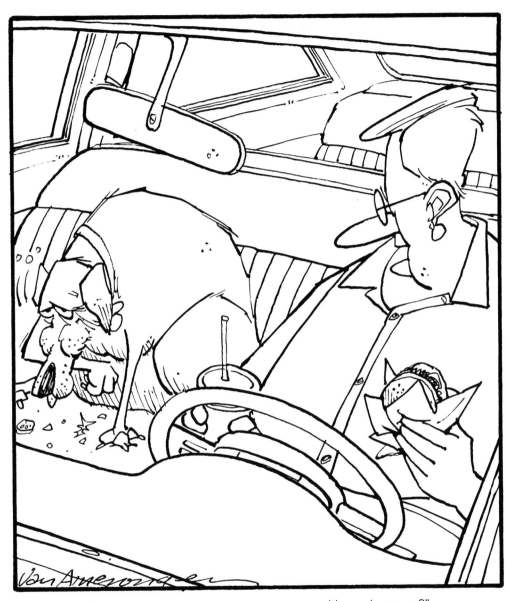

"Since when do we eat our wrappers with our burgers?"

"You're shrinking, Elliot."

"You could try reading, like other people!"

"What if I scale back the expectations I have for my body?" wonders Tom, with a flicker of hope.

Gloria is not immune to the joys of running free.

PERENNIAL FAVORITE, STERLING CONNERS, AT THIS YEARS NATIONAL TAXIDERMY FINALS.

"Wendell we need to do better entertainment planning".

Warren wonders, and not for the first time, if he's the right life form for his environment.

BY THE FOURTH TOSS TRISHA'S LACK OF CONDITIONING WAS APPARENT FOR ALL TO SEE

Gwen heads for her wine cellar.

Unlike some people she could name, Connie likes atmosphere with her reading..

"Come to think of it," thinks Allison, "I've been sagging south along a broad front myself."

"See, Millard, this is what I mean when I say you withhold!"

Winter enlivens Wendy.

I'LL TALK TO YOU ARTHUR, BUT NOT MR. MOJO!

"Lowell, you need to get out more!"

Ted is the most accommodating of pet owners.

There's another Natalie inside Natalie.

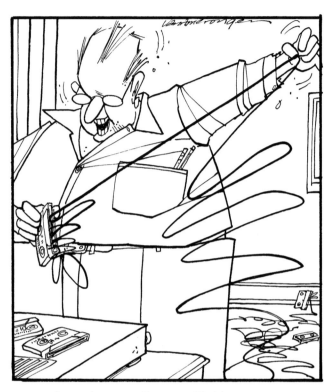

Larry loses patience with his anger
management tapes.

It occurs to Ted that the technology he's
being replaced with doesn't look all that
complicated.

Larry's losing confidence in nature.

"I have to get back to more loving thoughts," thinks Tammy.

Allen speaks with Nadine from his "corner of superiority.".

It occurs to Matthew that he's without an exit strategy.

TIME TO GET RID OF THE OAK, THINKS SANDRA

As Cynthia well knows, you control the nose and the rest will follow.

Be cutting edge, or lay back some?
Chet can't decide..

And just like that, Natalie exits the world
of signage.

The alarm bells are going off in Chuck's mind.

"I'm never going to try a new way of cleaning again!" grumbles Constance.

Gary micromanages his dog, Reggie

"Please, Jonathan, no monkey business tonight."

LITTLE SKIPPY ARBUCKLE LENDS AN ELEMENT OF HAZARD TO THE CENTRAL HALLWAY

Carl gives himself something to do on the way to his favorite chair.

Chet's "depth chart" helps him maintain order in the family.

Occasionally Kurt likes to do something just for himself.

"Clinton, have you seen any notebook paper with stuff about flying on them?"

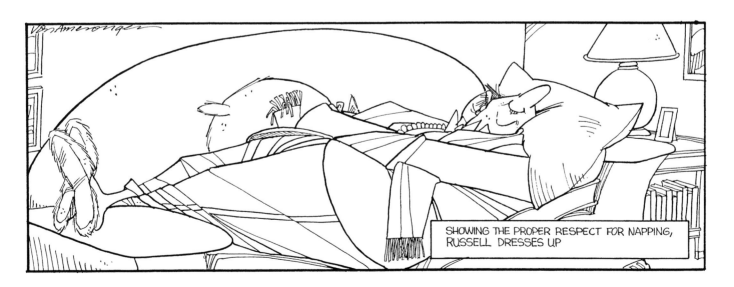

SHOWING THE PROPER RESPECT FOR NAPPING, RUSSELL DRESSES UP

Stephen dillydallies with Thunder.

"Ted, you know I don't care for it when you reposition yourself like this!"

YOU'VE NEVER BEGRUDED ME MY HOBBIES BEFORE, JANEL!...

Arthur stalls for time.

"It's a good day," thinks Larry, "to conduct one's self in an orderly manner."

Too bad Mason hasn't turned his considerable talents to something more useful.

"Oh, there you are!"

Warren gives his morning over completely to his own enrichment.

SIDNEY ENJOYS BUILDING HIS OWN CIGARS

After taking stock of his environment, Garrett decided to take a positive view.

It seems unlikely Bob's still in the running for this years " Happy Camper Award."

SUPPLE THOUGH HE MAY BE, WALKS WITH DAVIS ARE TEDIOUS

Somebody's got to stop Ted.

Audrey's thinking she can't expect much emotional support form Kenny today.

The company's wellness director shows signs of cracking.

As Arthur's evening at his carpentry bench progresses, he draws increasingly inward.

Times like these, Larry feels his blowgun was worth the cost.

Mr. Carney employs a personal advocate.

"Here's Cecil now!"

One look at the new guy, and Nelson knows he
needs to find another "Bermuda Shorts Club."

Hoping to locate aquatic life, Toby finds
only murkiness.

Jesse tells himself a real man should be able
to overcome a bad haircut.

"There's a surprise," mutters Stephanie.

Cindy is beginning to think Archie may be the emptiest of the vessels.

A short while ago, several of Gunner's primal urges got together and decided to let loose.

This is just the sort of thing that generally keeps Dorsey off city buses.

JEFFREY IS GLAD TO BE APOLITICAL

Roger spends the first part of the afternoon at a desktop rest shelter.

Marjorie wonders if Kenny might be one
martini away from having to give them up.

At home, however, Tony is quite the
high muckity-muck.

"Oh, no! The bridge is out! The bridge is out!".

Bud and Reggie can blow the better part of a morning reconnoitering the property line.

IT'S LITTLE WONDER THORNTON'S FISH, MICKY, IS SO SKITTISH

"You should put more thought in your creations."

"Walter, you stepped off in the wrong direction."

Aware of his poor choice of dress, Arthur attempts a
modicum of dignity while withdrawing.

"Gordon's taken up conducting."

Carrie forgets herself.

Trevor wonders if growing less active isn't being confused with growing more subtle.

Kevin's decided to go out and enjoy life.

THE NEIGHBORHOOD BRASS PLAYERS TAKE A BREAK

"Connor, your chiropractor is on the phone!"

"It's their dogged hopefulness that makes me not want to invite them over."

Of all the conversations Dale had to get stuck overhearing, it had to be one detailing the merits of various duffel bag designs.

Sometimes the quietest lives are visited by drama.

"I must set to work quickly," reasons Bob.

Marcie has taken up boogie-woogie blues.

Connie scuffs off some aggravation
on the back stoop.

Joseph manages to bum himself out.

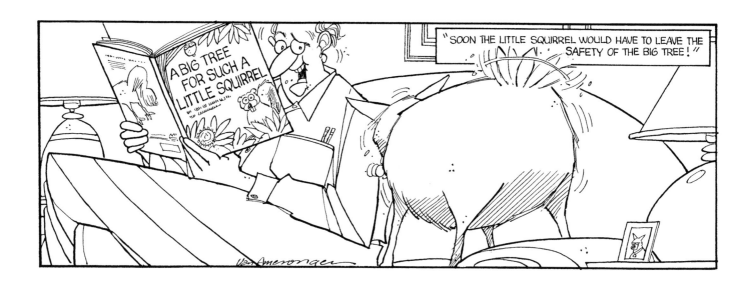

"I bet you have those little metal things on your heels, don't you?"

There are times when Ted's plaque
utterly stumps him.

"Douglas, after you cross the arroyo, come
get the phone!"

Stewart is surprised to find he'd eaten his report.

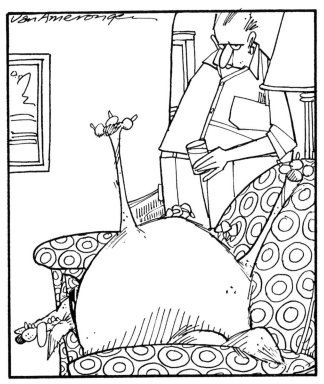

Kenny feels, keenly, the loss of his favorite spot.

MR. STACEY BELIEVES HE'S IDENTIFIED ANOTHER PROSPECTIVE CUSTOMER

EYE GLASSES 20% off

"I'm telling you I'm not a vampire!"

Terry laments the never-ending need for action as he ponders going up to get another latte.

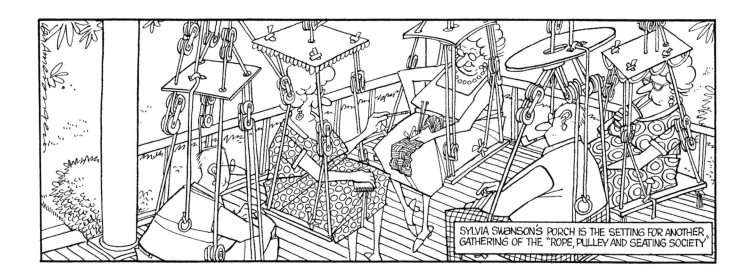

SYLVIA SWANSON'S PORCH IS THE SETTING FOR ANOTHER GATHERING OF THE "ROPE, PULLEY AND SEATING SOCIETY"

Neil has high hopes for Little Scuffy.

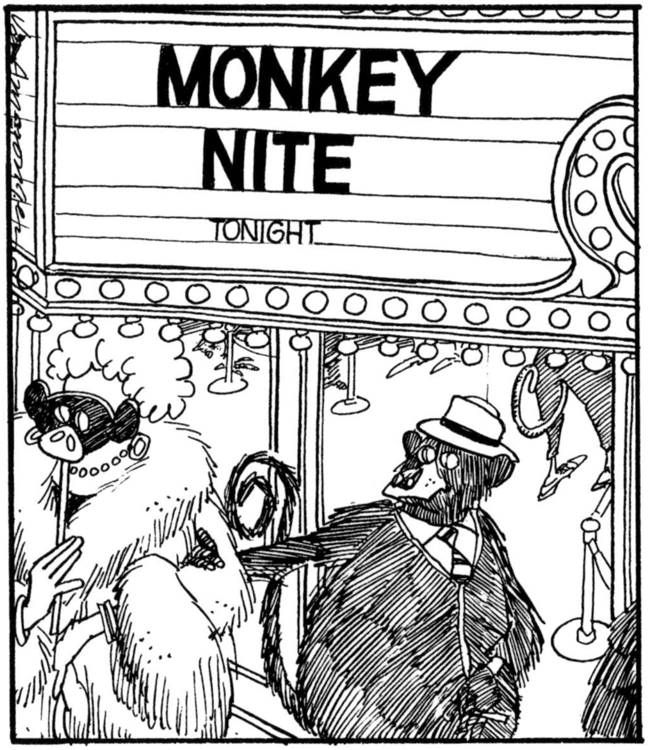
MONKEY
NITE
TONIGHT

Wouldn't you like to know what goes on in there?!

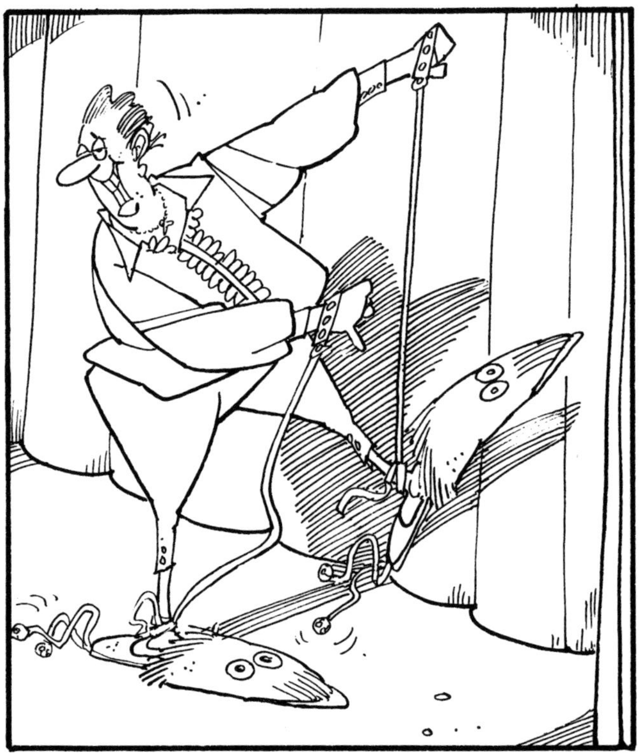

Todd has a chance to do well at this year's Carpet Slippers Invitational.

Meanwhile, over at the zoo, there's a changing of the guard.

FEEL BETTER ?!...

Celebrating Bird Day

Being keen on efficiency, Ben wonders if this is the most efficient place for his gloves.

NELSON BUILDS CONCRETE MICE IN HIS BASEMENT

Gary has an easy way with life.

As promotions continue to elude Jeffrey, he often hearkens back to this moment.

"Now what?!"

What you would expect from a weekly meeting of the Optimist Society.

Dick spot-checks the effectiveness of Dorothy's anti-anxiety medication.

AT HEART, MR. KRINKE, IS AN ADVENTURER

Dueling techies

Tonight, Aaron is joined by a
mysterious stranger.

"Marcia, here in my evaluation report, you keep referring to me as the project..."

Molly reaches the end of her
organizational capacity.

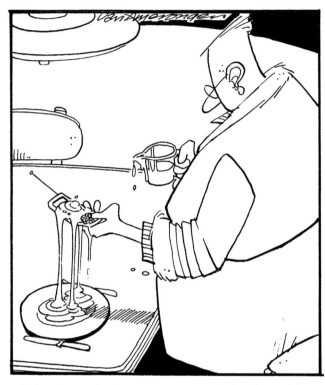

Believing cell phones to be capable of anything,
Sheldon tries for sourdough pancakes.

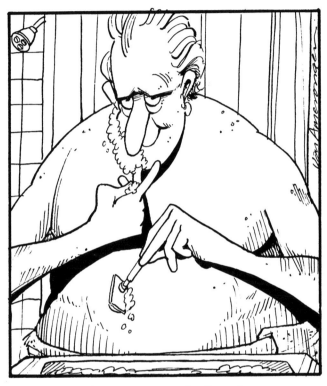

Lawrence you devil you!

Everyone in the office is, slowly but surely, being replaced by fruit.

Jason is utterly indifferent to discomfort.

"Sonya, you're wearing driving gloves."

More trouble in the produce department

Positive thinker, Little Rudy Callahan,
heads home.

The day begins with a degree of foreshadowing.

Toby has some unease over the new tea set.

Mr. Nivens reclaims the chair from kitty.

ROSEANNE IS CALMED BY THE ILLUSION OF ORDER

"Wait," thinks Scooter, "my supper isn't sitting all that well!"

Arlen tunes in and out at his leisure.

THE NEIGHBORS APPEAR TO HAVE TAKEN SOME SORT OF POSITION AGAINST ANGELA AND TREVOR

On rainy days, Todd leads the way with his wipers.

"This could get negative," thinks Charles.

Gordon's left wrist isn't going to be right for weeks..

Carl communes with nature..

Gerald experiences sympathy pains while eating ribs.

Warren has already fashioned a nice exoskeleton for Janice.

TED, TERRY AND MONTY BELONG TO A GROUP ADVOCATING THE USE OF DRESS SOCKS AS DECORATIVE ELEMENTS

"That's plenty of sun for one day, Everett!"

In a fit of optimism, Stan buys new hoses for next year.

The armored lifestyle is a challenge for Nathan.

"No more shaving cream for you, Boswell!"

Uncle Mickey does much of his ballooning in the kitchen.

BUD AND STACY HAVE A RACCOON PROBLEM

Dusty and Tom use dance to cement their relationship.

Edwin refuses to be intimidated by weather.

"You're right. It does give one a sense of power!"

"Are you gonna take all day?!"

Improved posture is another benefit of belonging to the Hood Ornament Club.

Stephen, Lyle and Chad have formed a gang.

Foraging for one's own food gives one a sense of accomplishment.

Ben allows his emotions full sway.

Garrett grinds away at trying to get his mind to take fanciful flight.

"Might this be one of those days,' wonders
Gracie, "when I'm made to feel inelegant?"

It's just the sort of poignancy one should
expect when one sings songs of the sea.

Some pets are getting closer and closer
to taking over.

"It's nice here by the creek, isn't it, Corky!"

It takes Herb forever to get to work.

173

"I'm gonna have to call you back."

Today is "new idea day" over at Eddie's house.

THERE'S SOMETHING A LITTLE UNNERVING ABOUT RUSTY AND SNYDER

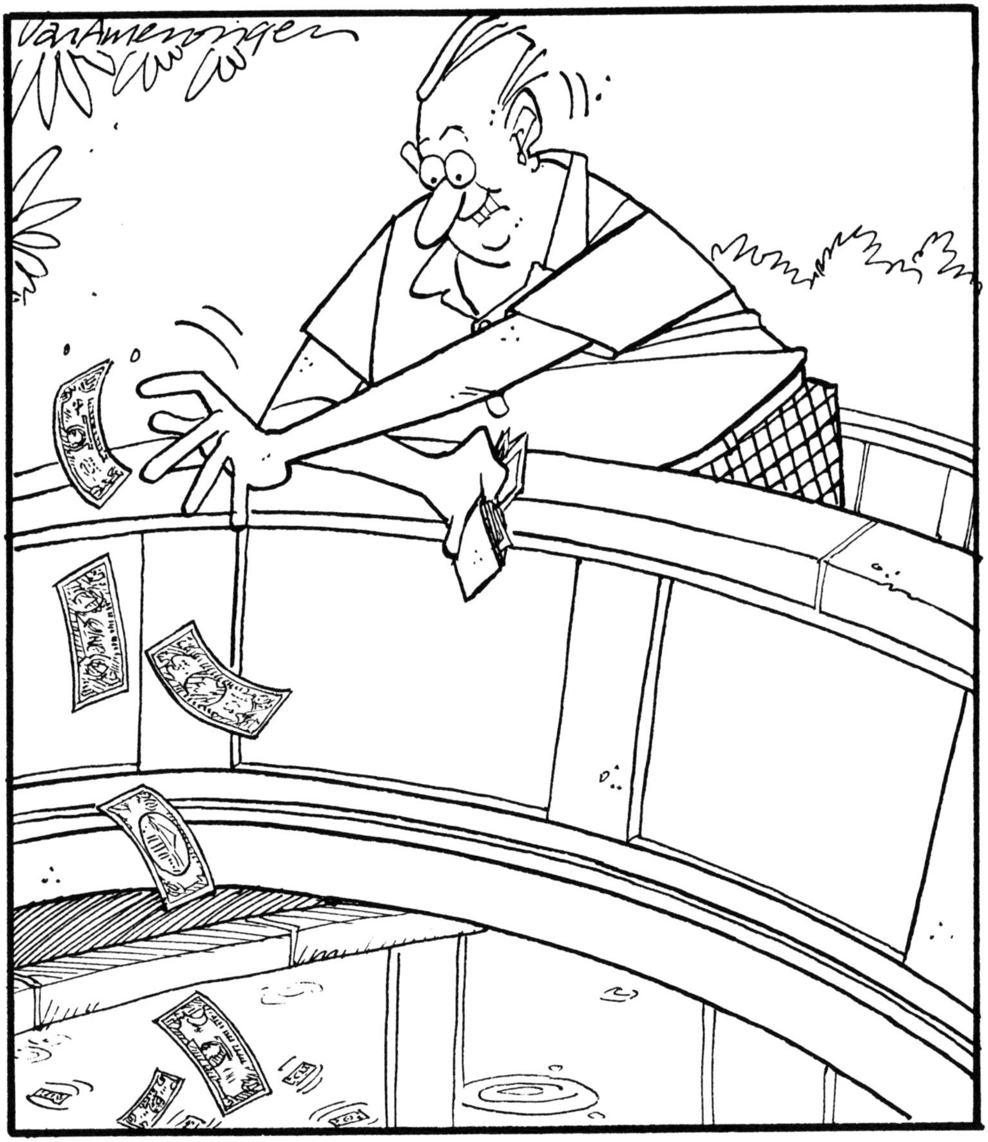
VanAmerongen

Monty's bad with money.

A coincidence in the making

David finds he's deviated from
the perpendicular.

When Allen's away, Vivian replaces him
with a 40-watt bulb.

As Rufus well knows, there's opportunity
in chaos.

Child entertainer Edwin Chambers

Turns out, Stephan did have an exit strategy.

Before reaching the office, Martin collects his thoughts.

"Lyle, I'm sorry your Rocket Club wasn't able to meet tonight."

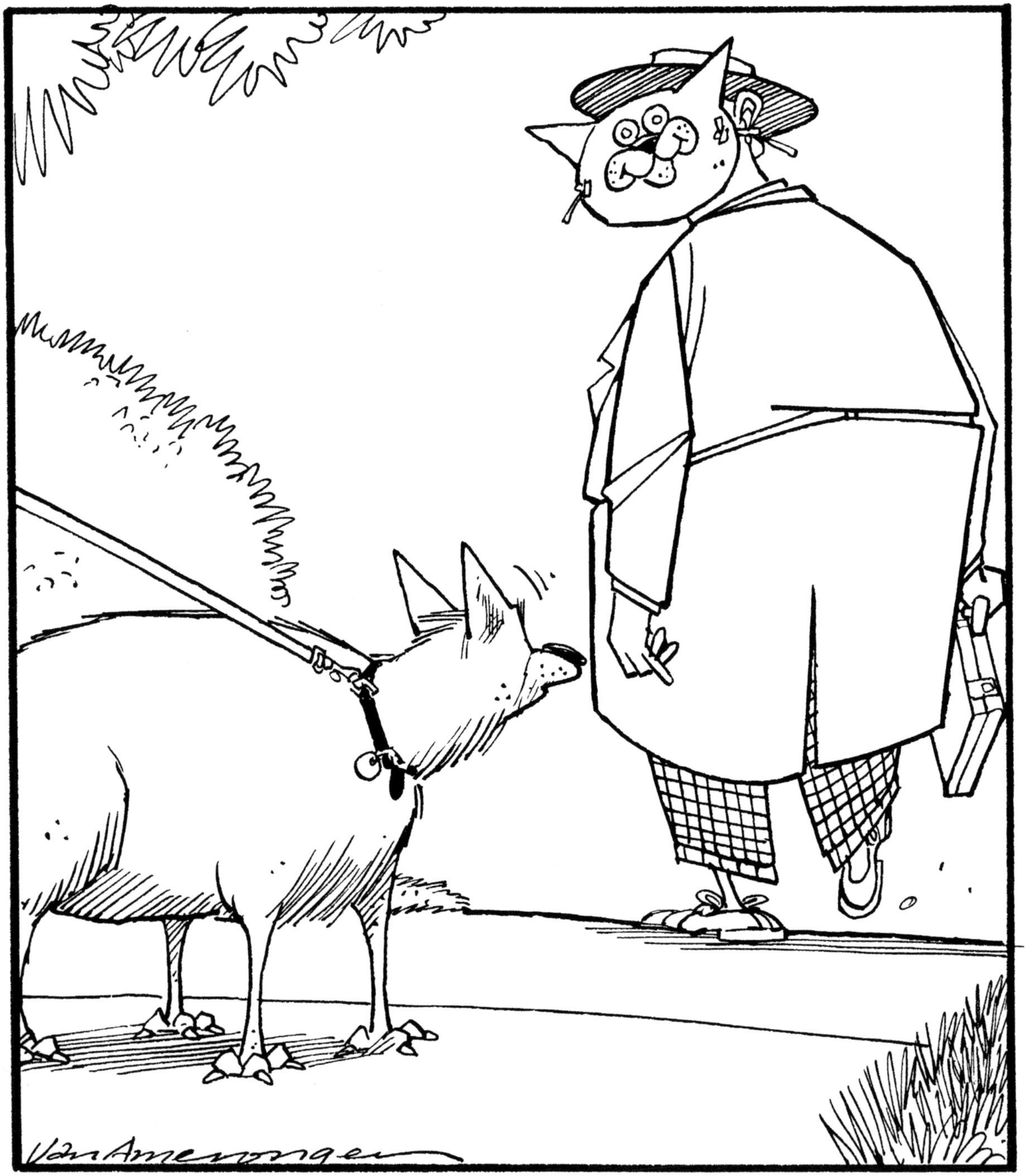
Van Amerongen

The End